Rashin Kheiriyeh was born in Iran and now lives in Washington, DC. She is one of the most outstanding Iranian illustrators working today. She has been awarded the Golden Apple of Bratislava and was selected for the 2013 Bologna Book Fair Illustrators Exhibit and a 2014 IBBY Honor. In 2023, Rashin was nominated for the Astrid Lindgren Memorial Award for outstanding contributions to children's literature. Among her many books are "Two Parrots," "There Was an Old Lady Who Swallowed a Fly," and "The Seven Voyages of Sinbad the Sailor"—her first books published in the United States.

Rumi (1207–1273) was a poet, an Islamic scholar, and Sufi mystic. He wrote his extensive work mostly in Persian / Farsi. To this day, his poetry enjoys great popularity worldwide and appears in new translations.

For women, life, and freedom—R. K.

Text and illustrations copyright © 2023 by Rashin Kheiriyeh

Published in the United States, Great Britain, Canada, Australia, and New Zealand in 2024 by NorthSouth Books, Inc., an imprint of NordSüd Verlag AG, CH-8050 Zürich, Switzerland. German translation of English text published in 2023 by NordSüd Verlag AG, CH-8050 Zürich, Switzerland.

Distributed in the United States by NorthSouth Books, Inc., New York 10016.
Library of Congress Control Number: 2023934397
ISBN: 978-0-7358-4544-2 (trade edition)
1 3 5 7 9 • 10 8 6 4 2
Printed in Latvia

Rumi

Poet of Joy and Love

Rashin Kheiriyeh

North
South

It began with a leaf
yellow and orange
falling from the tree.

On September 30, 1207—that is a long time ago—a child was born
on a crisp and colorful autumn day in Iran.
They called him Rumi.
Everyone welcomed little Rumi into the world.

Growing up, Rumi loved to play and dance in the garden. He ran after butterflies and delighted in the scent of roses and the songs of the birds.

Little Rumi loved to feed the birds
and watch them fly around.
His favorite bird was a hoopoe,
the symbol of wisdom.

Rumi had so many questions. He wondered who had created this beautiful world.

His father answered his questions patiently and taught him what he knew. One day, his father said to Rumi, "Learn generosity from the sun. It lights the world every day and asks for nothing in return."
Did Rumi know that he would meet the sun in person one day?
Not yet.

As Rumi grew older, his favorite thing was to read books. He was excited to meet Attar, a great Persian poet. Attar gave him his epic poem called "The Conference of the Birds." The book had a picture of a giant bird on the cover.

"I love birds! Thank you, Attar," Rumi said.

"Read it and search for the deeper meaning. One day you will shine and illuminate the world like the sun," Attar said to young Rumi.

Rumi opened the book.
The story was about a mythical bird called Sīmurgh.
Hoopoe and hundreds of other birds of all kinds had to cross seven stages, or valleys, to find Sīmurgh, whom they wanted as their king. It was a difficult journey, and at the end only thirty birds could make it. But when the birds finally reached their destination, they realized that they were actually the Sīmurgh. By flying all together, they made a giant bird. To this day, Sīmurgh means "Thirty Birds" in Persian—sī means "thirty,"and Murgh means "bird."

Rumi closed his eyes to imagine it. When he opened them again it was as if he saw the bird take flight.

Years passed. Rumi moved to Turkey with his family. He was just a young man when he became a well-known scholar and teacher like his father and grandfather. His students and followers gathered from near and far to listen to him and take part in his classes.

Despite all his success, Rumi was not happy. Something was missing in his heart.

One day, Rumi was passing by the bazaar when a stranger said
hello to him. "Salam, Rumi."
The stranger was a Persian spiritual teacher who traveled the world
to find God.
His name was Shams, which means "the sun."
"I traveled the world, met many people, and collected their stories.
Today I am here to hear your story, Rumi," Shams said.

Rumi and Shams talked for days and hours.
Soon they became close friends.
Rumi was inspired by Shams.
Shams was a sun, shining in Rumi's heart and mind.

But Rumi's students weren't happy about all the attention that Shams got from Rumi. They were jealous.

Rumi was happy to have found a good friend.
"Friendship is the bridge between you and everything," said Shams.
Rumi agreed, and danced Sama to thank God.
Sama means "listening."
He raised his hands to the sky, spinning, spinning, spinning in a circle
to celebrate unity and friendship.

He danced like a floating leaf
falling from a tree in autumn.

Sadly, Rumi's students asked Shams to leave Rumi alone.
They wanted their master for themselves once again.
They forced Shams to leave the town without saying good-bye to Rumi.
He disappeared on the horizon like the sunset.

Rumi was very sad to lose his dear friend.
He searched everywhere for Shams, but he wasn't able to find him.
Rumi grew silent and depressed.

Rumi's students regretted what they had done.
They tried to find Shams to bring him back home,
but Shams was nowhere to be found.
Rumi remembered Attar's poem, "The Conference of the Birds."
Like the birds searching together, Rumi became what he
was searching for.

"WE ARE WHAT WE SEEK!
I AM THE SĪMURGH!" Rumi thought.

That night, Rumi saw his mother in a dream. She was wearing a beautiful dress and held a feather pen in her hand. Rumi was a child again. She gave the pen to Rumi and whispered, "Write, my son. You will find what you are looking for. Share your stories of friendship with everyone you love."

Rumi began to write—for days and nights. Word after word. He merged letters like drops of rain merge in the ocean. And he finished his poetic masterpiece "The Masnavi."
His book was inspired by his friendship with Shams and everyday tales. Everyone loved his book—especially children. Soon his book was translated into many languages. And Rumi became one of the greatest writers of all time.

More than anything, Rumi loved telling stories to children.
"To me nothing in the world is as precious as a genuine smile,
especially from a child," Rumi said.

Children gathered around Rumi to listen to a story.
"Sit, be still, and listen," Rumi said.
The children sat quietly and listened carefully.
"Once upon a time, there was a merchant who had a pretty parrot. . . . "

Rumi found peace in writing. He forgave his students for their mistake.
"You are the SĪMURGH of love and liberty! Unity is strength!"
Rumi said to them.

And he danced Sama to thank God.

Children danced with him. They opened their arms; raised their little hands
to the sky; and spinning, spinning, spinning, they flew like birds.

Rumi

Author's note

I love Rumi. He is my favorite Persian poet of all time. I grew up with his books in Iran. My mom used to tell me his tales when I was little. I wrote this book to celebrate his 750th birthday in 2023. I wrote it for the readers who are wondering who Rumi was and how he became a great poet that everyone loves. I hope this book will encourage you to go ahead and read Rumi's tales.

Rumi was a religious man, but after he met Shams his life changed—he found God in love.

Rumi left us many valuable writings to read and enjoy. He is alive in our hearts and minds as long as we read his books.

"The best religion is to make friends with all the people of the world," Rumi said.

Rumi connects faith in God with universal love. It makes him so deeply human, and the message embraces us all.

And this is what I love about him.

—Rashin Kheiriyeh

Rumi 1207–1273

Jalāl al-Dīn Muhammad Rūmī (also known as Mevlânâ/Mawlānā) was born on September 30, 1207, in Balkh Province—originally part of Iran in the thirteenth century—but now part of Afghanistan. He was a Persian poet, an Islamic teacher, and a Sufi mystic.

Rumi's works are mostly written in Persian (or Farsi) with others written in Turkish, Arabic, and Greek.

"The Masnavi" is considered one of the great works in Persian language. Rumi's extensive poem consists of 24,000 verses, and it is full of tales about animals and people from all over the world, such as "The Tale of the Merchant and the Parrots," "The Cunning Tailor," "The Man Who Learned the Language of Animals," "The Young Man and the Bear," and so many more.

Rumi died on December 17, 1273. His tomb is located in Konya, Turkey. Every year many people visit there to see the whirling dervishes performance known as a Sama to celebrate Rumi's life.

Rumi's poetry has been widely translated. His poetry remains immensely popular, especially in the United States and South Asia.

As you read in the book, Sama is a Sufi ceremony performed as part of meditation and prayer. It represents a mystical journey of a person's spiritual ascent through mind and love to perfection.

Dancers wear long white robes with full skirts. On the dancers' heads sit tall conical felt hats called sikke. In 2008, UNESCO confirmed the Mevlevi Sama Ceremony in Turkey as one of the Masterpieces of the Oral and Intangible Heritage of Humanity.

The story about the Sīmurgh conveys the message that the beginning point and the final point of the journey are the same. What the birds see when they reach the end of their long and challenging journey is none other than themselves. This represents the Sufis' full knowledge of themselves spiritually and physically.

Selected bibliography: Attar. *The Conference of the Birds*. Translated by Sholeh Wolpe. W. W. Norton & Company; Reprint edition. 2018. Barks, Coleman. *The Essential Rumi*—New Expanded Edition. Harper Collins, 2004. Rumi. *Fihi Ma Fihi*. Negah Edition. Iran. 2022. Rumi. *The Masnavi Mnavi*. Aban Edition. Iran. 2016 (In Farsi/English)